God hears

Notes for parents and other adult readers

Sitting down to read a book with a young child is a special privilege, and helping them take early steps in getting to know their world, themselves and God is even more special. However this book is not just intended to be read, but to be a springboard for helping children learn throughout the day (Deuteronomy 6:4-7; Psalm 145:3-7). Here are a few tips to help you adapt your reading and help their learning go beyond these pages:

For really little ones: In this book, we lead up to a generalization (we can talk to God anywhere and anytime and he hears us) by starting with specifics (e.g. inside, daytime). You can make the transition to your child's life by making it even more specific (e.g. "We can pray here in this room.") Even though we can pray anytime, you can also explain that it's still good to have a regular time each day when you pray. Keep prayers simple and short.

For bigger ones: You can use this book to help your child learn to pray themselves and help them cultivate dependence on God in everyday life. Talk to your child about how they could pray in response to things (for themselves or for others). At first, you can model short, simple prayers. Or you could begin a prayer (e.g. "Please God help...") for them to name the person or the situation. Then you could talk about what to pray and either you pray or you suggest what they can pray. Over time they might pray simple prayers themselves.

Other Bible passages to look at: Psalm 116:2; 1 Thessalonians 5:17; 1 John 5:14.

Making books for/with your child: Photograph your child and people they know (or an older child can draw). Put the pictures in a small album that can be used as a 'prayer book' when praying.

Pray: Thank God for listening to our prayers. Pray that God will help you both talk to God through the day. Ask God to help you love other people by praying for them. There are other books in this series about prayer too.

For more thoughts and tips, see www.teachinglittleones.com/bflo.

GOD HEARS © MATTHIAS MEDIA 2016

Matthias Media (St Matthias Press Ltd ACN 067 558 365) | Email: info@matthiasmedia.com.au
Internet: www.matthiasmedia.com | Please visit our website for current postal and telephone contact information.

All Scripture quotations in this publication are from the Good News Translation in Today's English Version - Second Edition Copyright © 1992 by American Bible Society. Used by permission.

ISBN 978 1 925424 03 4

Cover design and typesetting by Karen Tse.

Photos: See www.teachinglittleones.com/bflo/photocredits.html

God wants me to talk to him.
I can't see him but he can hear me.

I can talk to God in the daytime
and he hears me.

I can talk to God in the nighttime.
I can talk to God anytime and he hears me.

I can talk to God when I'm inside
and he hears me.

I can talk to God outside and he hears me.
I can talk to God wherever I am.

I can talk to God quietly by myself
and he hears me.

I can talk to God with my family and with my friends. God always hears us.

I can talk to God when I'm happy
and he hears me.

I can talk to God when I'm sad or when I'm sick.
God always hears me.

I can say 'Thank you God'.
I can say 'Please God help me'. I can say 'Please God help my family and my friends'.

I can also say 'Sorry God'.

God's book, the Bible, says God hears me
when I talk to him. Talking to God is called prayer.

"I love the Lord, because he hears me;
he listens to my prayers."

Psalm 116 verse 1

Thank you God that you want me to talk to you.
Thank you that you always hear me.